Argyll

A *Strong* *Start* In LANGUAGE

Ruth Beechick

D0032141

arrow press

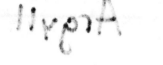

Other books in this series of *The Three R's* include:

An Easy Start in Arithmetic
A Home Start in Reading

More homeschooling books by this author include:

You CAN Teach Your Child Successfully: Grades 4-8
Dr. Beechick's Homeschool Answer Book
The Language Wars and other Writings for Homeschoolers
GENESIS: Finding Our Roots
Adam and His Kin: The Lost History of their Lives and Times

Printed in the United States of America
Distributed by Education Services
8825 Blue Mountain Drive, Golden CO 80403

Contents

The Powerful Natural Method

Parent, you may not realize it, but you are an excellent language teacher. You can prove that by the speech of your child. Think of how much language he learned by age five or so. Don't you wish you spoke a new foreign language as well? If you did, you could go to that country and ask directions, make purchases, or get acquainted with people. In short, you would feel fairly competent in the language.

That's the amazing accomplishment of your young child. How did you teach him? By using the powerful natural method. This manual will show you how to extend the natural method from spoken language to written language. With this method your child's writing ability will grow in great leaps, just as his speaking ability grew in the preschool years.

The method is not new or experimental. It is an old and proven method, probably as old as writing itself. Great writers have used it, and you have already used it with your child. But once children reach school age, we tend to shed the natural method for a slower, artificial method. Our society thinks grammar books or language books somehow carry the secret of good writing, but few of them do.

What is the natural method of learning to write? Before defining it, let's think back to the child's learning of speech. How did he learn to speak? By listening and speaking. The baby at first listened to you, he imitated sounds and words, and from there he rapidly grew into a competent speaker. This is no secret known only in the ivy halls of teacher colleges. It is known in every house on the block. And if that sounds like a miracle, attribute it to the innate abilities God planted in the child. Speech is learned by listening and speaking.

Now, what is the parallel for written language? It is reading and writing. We might state the analogy this way: Listening and speaking are to spoken language what reading and writing are to written language. If people ask you how children learn to write, here is the short, short definition to give them: Children learn to write by writing.

But you need a longer definition than that in order to make practical use of this powerful natural method in your teaching. For that, we must examine some features of this system.

What You Do in a Lesson

Probably your child's first writing lesson was when you printed his name and he traced it or copied it. Or maybe you started even earlier with one letter instead of a word. This kind of copying is what happens in many lessons for a young child. Later, the copying gives way to writing from dictation. Copying and dictating are the two basic lesson activities in the natural method. Just as the child learned to speak by copying your correct speech, so he learns to write by copying fine writing.

Jack London tells how he taught himself to write his famous adventure stories. Even if they had summer writing conferences in his day, he could not have afforded to go to one. But he stumbled onto the natural method, which obviously helped his career more than a conference would have anyway. London spent days upon days in the San Francisco Public Library hand copying good literature that the librarian recommended to him.

Benjamin Franklin tells in his autobiography how he taught himself to write. It began when he admired some writing in a British periodical, *The Spectator*. The essays with their closely reasoned arguments caught his fancy, and he wanted to write like that. So he outlined essays, put his outlines aside for a few days, and later tried to rewrite an original article by following his outline. He compared his writing with the model to see where he fell short. Then he repeated with the same essay again or tried another essay, improving his writing all the while. Later, he had the pleasure of thinking he sometimes did a portion better than the writer he was modeling.

These three examples indicate the broad range of levels you can use with your child when you plan writing lessons—all the way from carefully forming letters of a child's name to reconstructing an essay from an outline. Copy, dictate, compare, repeat. These and similar activities can be used in any combination in your daily writing lessons.

A caution is in order here: The natural method sounds simple in theory and your lessons may seem easy to plan, but do not be deceived. Writing is hard work. Some days your child will complain, "Do I have to write today?" "Yes," you should answer, "you have to write every day." That means every school day, except for field trip days or other occasions when writing gets squeezed out by something better.

The following list gives in brief the levels of difficulty from easy to hard that you can use in your lesson plans.

1. Trace a model letter or word.
2. Copy a model word or sentence.
3. Write a sentence from slow dictation, getting all the help necessary to make it correct.
4. Write a familiar sentence from dictation given at normal speed and expression. Compare. Write again.
5. Write an unfamiliar sentence from dictation. Compare. Write again.
6. Study a paragraph. Write as it is dictated sentence by sentence in normal expression. Compare and correct errors.
7. Write an unfamiliar paragraph from dictation, deciding from the expression how it should be punctuated. Compare. Talk about any differences between your writing and the model. Learn from these differences.
8. Write from dictation a variety of passages which are longer than a paragraph—dialogues, descriptions, news stories, and others. Compare. Learn.
9. Review by repeating two or three times any lesson in which you made too many errors. (If you keep on making many errors, find easier sentences or paragraphs.)
10. Make notes on a passage of writing that you like, and put the notes away for a few days. Then try to rewrite the passage from your notes. Compare with the model. What did you do well? Where will you do better next time? Repeat, using the same model or a new one.
11. Find a description, or poem, or any short piece of writing that you like. Use it as a pattern to write something of your own.
12. Find a letter to the editor or other piece of writing that you disagree with. Write your answer.
13. When you have something to say, decide what form you will use—essay, poem, letter, or other—and write your thoughts for someone else to read.

You can see from this list that the range of difficulty can take you from kindergarten or first grade through the Benjamin Franklin level. Another way to vary the difficulty is through the choice of content for writing. For instance, number 11, which is high on the difficulty list, could be adapted to primary children by selecting a nursery rhyme or other model the child likes and letting him imitate it and try to make his own. Or for older writers, an existing set of by-laws could provide a model for writing by-laws for a new organization. Number 13, also, can be used by primary children or by their parents.

Thus, the levels should not be used too rigidly in your teaching. But they can give you general guidelines for helping your child progress in his writing.

Proven Track Record

Another feature of the powerful natural method of teaching writing is that it has a long proven track record. Not only did Jack London and Benjamin Franklin use it, but so also did countless other famous and ordinary writers of past generations.

Past generations of American students were raised on it. They wrote in more complex sentences and often with more organized thoughts because they studied from those kinds of models. In some places or eras of our past, children were tutored, and the natural method could easily be used. After schools grew large and graded, workbooks came into use as a way for teachers to manage large groups of children. And workbooks diluted the task of writing. Though the natural method could work well in classrooms, and does in some schools, filling in blanks too often substituted for real writing.

Now with a revival of home tutoring there is opportunity to discard workbooks and do real writing again. Mothers across the country are rediscovering the natural method. One mother read in a McGuffey reader that copying and dictating methods were good to use. She tried it and was amazed at the results. Her child, she said, could write anything he wanted to. Other mothers discover the method simply because it is the natural one. They start by showing a child to write his name, and go on from there.

So throughout American history, right up to the present day, many people have used and are using the natural method with excellent results. Those who are just hearing about it say, "It must be good because it sounds so sensible."

From Whole to Part

An old debate among curriculum makers involves the whole-versus-part question. Should you teach something piece by piece by piece until the pieces add up to a whole? Or should you start with some kind of understandable whole and teach the pieces through it? The reason the debate goes on so long is that neither method is right for every topic and for every time. The wholes and the parts do not separate as neatly as curriculum planners would like.

In language teaching, what is a whole? As the method is described in this manual, a whole is any meaningful piece of language—from a word or sentence up to an essay or even longer passage of writing. This is written language in its natural setting.

What are the parts of language? They are innumerable and include all kinds of grammar matters; punctuation, capitalization and other mechanics; usage; vocabulary; spelling; meaning; forms; and on and on.

Now, the big question is: Is it better to move from whole to parts or from parts to whole? The natural method, the method of learning to write by studying and doing writing, is basically a whole-to-part method.

Teaching of the grammar parts has been researched extensively. If you tested any group of children to find who knows a lot of grammar and who knows only a little grammar, you would find that the grammar scores do not correlate with quality of writing. Children who know the most grammar are not necessarily better writers. The parts do not add up to the desired whole.

But moving in the opposite direction does work. That is, students who are good writers can learn grammar better than students who are poor writers. Grammar is not a way to good writing; it is a tool that good writers use to analyze writing, to justify doing something this way instead of that way, and so forth.

When your child learned to speak, he learned more grammar than you ever thought of teaching him. Even a five-year-old uses statements, questions, commands and exclamations. In other words, he knows the major types of sentences. He forms most sentences with subjects and predicates. He uses verbs in both present and past tense forms. Many other details of grammar could be added to the list. All this without a formal grammar lesson!

Children's mistakes can make us aware of how much grammar they have absorbed. "I knowed the cake was in there," shows that the child can form past tense by adding *ed* to a verb. The problem in the cake sentence is that the child hasn't learned yet about irregular verbs—at least the verb *know*.

One young preschooler said, "It isn't any more rain." If we were to correct him we might say, "*There* isn't any more rain." The words *it* and *there* are sometimes used in this manner as anticipatory subjects, in this case to anticipate the real subject, rain. *It* is also used as an impersonal pronoun, as in "It isn't raining any more." What sophisticated grammar this child almost had in his grasp!

The learning method which children use for spoken language works as well for written language. You can teach the parts of capitalization, punctuation, spelling, sometimes grammar, and numerous other matters day by day in the dictation and copying lessons. Some of them you will consciously teach. Many others the child will learn without your conscious effort. He will learn from the good language models he studies, in the same natural way he learned to speak.

Efficiency is a correlate of learning from wholes. When your child studies from a workbook or textbook in which parts chosen by a curriculum planner are laid out in some kind of order, it is inevitable that the child will meet parts he already knows or parts he cannot yet understand. It also is inevitable that he will learn some matters that he does not yet need in his writing, so he will forget them. When your child learns any part because he needs it to get his dictation correct, the learning is stronger.

A part-to-whole lesson on nouns, for instance, may teach a definition of nouns, list some nouns, and then give sentences for underlining the nouns. In this, the noun lesson is predominant and whatever meaning or significance the sentences may have is only incidental. But a whole-to-part lesson could begin with a paragraph from a history book which you chose because of its meaning and significance. Say that the child writes it from dictation and does well, so you decide to add on an incidental lesson about nouns. Discussing nouns in the passage gives an extra boost to vocabulary learning. You could notice proper nouns and titles, such as General Washington. In such a lesson, meaning is uppermost, and the noun learning incidental. But even in its incidental position it is stronger learning about nouns than in the other lesson.

In summary, a feature of the natural method is that it moves from whole to part. This kind of learning is stronger and more efficient. It is proven. It works.

Leads to Creativity

If you teach language by the natural method, sooner or later some friend is sure to say, "It stifles creativity to have the child write from models instead of using his own creative ideas." Our society is so obsessed with creativity that people want children to be creative before they have any knowledge or skill to be creative with. In using this natural method you will be providing your child with knowledge and skill. Whenever he has an idea for a story, poem, letter, or anything of his own, let him write it. Encourage such creative urges when they poke up their heads. But in between times, get back to the daily dictation lessons. There is no better way to give your child a strong foundation for his own creative writing.

Listen to a musician advising young composers how to learn from the great masters: "As a technical exercise he may copy down the soprano line ... and attempt to supply the accompanying parts, comparing his result with that of the master. He will find that with practice he is able to duplicate the original accompaniments or supply alternatives which are equally proficient technically" (Harold Shapero in *The Creative Process* edited by Brewster Ghiselin). Does that sound like the Benjamin Franklin method of writing?

Every master painter had followers who painted imitations of his works as a way to become painters in their own right. That is why art lovers today sometimes have difficulty figuring out whether a particular painting is an original or a copy.

Your child should not be required to reinvent the wheel, so to speak, in learning to write. Let him learn from fine writing models; then his creativity can begin at higher levels. An occasional fifth grader has a novel in her head and at every opportunity sneaks out her manuscript to write a few more paragraphs. An occasional third or fourth grader keeps diaries without anyone assigning such a project. Many first graders, excited that they can now write and spell a few words, want to make up their own stories.

It works well to let children write their own material when they have something in their heads to write. But it does not work well to regularly require original writing. Too many school children have written "What I Did on My Summer Vacation" and "What I Would Do if I Had a Million Dollars."

The natural method frees you from having to find or think up writing topics to try to motivate your child to do original writing. It is relatively easy to find passages for copying and dictation. They can come from any reading lesson or from science, history, poetry—in fact, from anything meaningful to the child that you think is worth his time.

So you have an answer for friends who worry about creativity: "The natural method leads to higher levels of creativity than other methods."

Grade-Level Guidelines

The grade-level lists that follow are distilled from major language textbooks so you can see what the majority of schools purport to teach. I think they are good lists for homeschool guidance except for the grammar sections in second and third grades. It is better to wait until about seventh grade when children are fairly good writers, and then have some units on grammar.

In this advice, I am separating grammar from usage and from writing mechanics. Strictly speaking, grammar is the study of the parts of speech and the parts of sentences. As mentioned earlier, much research has shown that knowledge of grammar does not correlate at all with good writing. So reverse the order in your teaching. Teach your children first to write well and then teach them some grammar. They will understand it at that time, and may even enjoy it, not having been burned out previously with years of useless grammar study.

Young children should learn the mechanics. The mechanics are punctuation, capitalization and other details needed for writing but not needed for speaking.

If you delay grammar, don't worry about "gaps" or achievement tests, or keeping up with the schools. If your children are immersed in language—hearing and reading good books, conversing, and writing—they will do fine in the tests. No test asks them to underline a verb or to find a preposition. Any student with a good ear for language can answer the kinds of questions they will meet on the tests. And don't worry that your child is missing something he might have gotten in school. If you look in a textbook for some of the grammar items listed, you will find only one or two lessons on them. Or sometimes an item has no lesson, but is included briefly on a page that teaches another topic.

In other words, those scope and sequence charts seem primarily for impressing textbook selection committees, or maybe parents, and the curriculum writers know better than to teach a lot of grammar to primary children.

With the natural method, you will have no problem teaching the non-grammar items on these lists.

First Grade

Oral Language. Speak clearly. Show courtesy. Tell about something, keeping to the subject.

Listening. Listen for details, sequence, directions, rhyme.

Writing. Write sentences which together tell a story. Write a simple invitation or announcement.

Punctuation. Use periods after statements and abbreviations. Use question marks after questions.

Second Grade

Oral Language. Grow in clarity of expression and in conversation ability, giving and taking turns. Expand oral vocabulary.

Listening. Give attention to teaching and other presentations that are within child's understanding level. Expand in vocabulary. (People always understand more words than they use in speech.)

Writing. Understand a wider variety of writing purposes: descriptions, explanations, news stories, directions, poems, stories, plays, letters, and so forth. Grow in ability to write appropriately for these purposes. Edit own writing and find most problems needing correcting.

Punctuation. Use comma in friendly letter greetings and closings and in series within a sentence. Use apostrophe to show missing letters in contractions and to show possession.

Capitalization. Capitalize sentence beginnings, greetings in letters, proper nouns, main words of titles.

Grammar. Is introduced to the subject-predicate order of most sentences. Begin to learn about nouns, verbs, pronouns, and perhaps coordinating conjunction (and) and articles (a, an, the). Some grammars speak of "determiners" which signal nouns. These include the articles as well as possessive pronouns and other words which precede nouns (his book, that book).

Usage. Use *a* before a consonant and *an* before a vowel. Do not use double negatives. Name self last (he and I). Learn when to use lie, lay, ate, eaten, and a few other troublesome words.

Vocabulary. Understand about antonyms and synonyms, compound words, and homophones (words which sound alike, such as *their* and *there*).

Study Skills. Learn to use indexes and tables of contents. Learn to put three or four words into ABC order by the first and second letters. Learn about the children's section of the local library. Where is the fiction? The non-fiction? The easy books? Are there tapes or toys or other items besides books to check out?

Third Grade

Oral. Take part in discussions, use the telephone, show courtesy, tell things in order, describe accurately, give directions and instructions.

Listening. Understand necessary details, sequence, messages. Recognize and make rhymes.

Writing. Write good sentences and prepare book reports, stories, and friendly letters (including addressing the envelope). Choose a good title, keep to the subject, and tell enough to make the writing interesting. Indent at the beginning of a paragraph.

Punctuation. Use periods after abbreviations and initials, and after statements, commands, and requests. Use question marks after questions. Use commas between city and state, in dates, after greeting and closing of letter.

Capitalization. Capitalize I; the first word of sentences; the first word of greetings and closings in letters; names and titles of people, names of places and other proper nouns; main words in the titles of books, poems, stories, and reports.

Grammar. Understand that a statement has two main parts—the part that names and the part that tells something about the thing named. (Complete subject and complete predicate—sometimes called noun phrase and verb phrase.)

Nouns: They name people, places, and things. Learn about singular, plural, common, proper, and possessive nouns.

Pronouns: I, you, she, he, it, we, you, and they can take the place of nouns in the subject part of sentences. Me, you, her, him, it, us, and them can take the place of nouns in the predicate part of sentences.

Verbs: There are action verbs and being verbs. Add *ed* to form past tense of many verbs. Some verbs form past tense other ways.

Adjectives: These words describe people, places, and things.

Adverbs: These words tell when, where, or how about the verb in a sentence.

Conjunction: Sometimes *and* connects two parts of a subject (Mom and I, Bob and Ben).

Usage. Use correctly: is, are, give, gave, given, did, done, saw, seen, came, come. Name self last (him and me, not me and him.)

Study Skills. Use a dictionary, finding words and their meanings, and using the guide words for greater speed. Use the library indexing system (even if it's computerized) to find a book. Read simple maps.

Spelling

Spelling is automatically integrated with writing when you use the natural method of teaching writing. Thus there is no need to set up a separate subject called "spelling."

In fact, when we realize that young children are trying to learn letters and sounds and reading and writing and capitalizing and penmanship and numerous other language details besides spelling, we could decide that it is overload for many children, and spelling is the aspect that we could treat lightly while we focus on the reading and writing. Primary teachers understand that when children are required to have perfect spelling, they will write with a more impoverished vocabulary and with less creativity, so they enjoy the children's invented spelling. This shows what phonics they have learned and it shows they are trying to spell correctly.

A good time to tackle spelling hard is about fourth grade reading level when children are reading fluently and have built a good visual foundation for how words should look. In the meantime, teach bits of spelling as they fit into daily writing.

Two major school approaches are described in this chapter, and then follows the personalized approach that is much more efficient for homeschoolers. First, four principles which apply to all of spelling.

1. Good spelling is an attitude. Years of memorizing words do not add up to good spelling unless a student cares. And students who care are produced by teachers who care. Somewhere down in the list of life priorities you have to add spelling because, like it or not, the world judges our education largely on our spelling and writing. Let's hope that school officials do not receive letters that say, "I beleive that God gave parants the duty to educate there own children."

2. Good spelling includes the skill of knowing when to check on a word. A strong case can be made that this is *the* most important spelling skill, yet it is the most neglected. We get so busy with memorizing words and giving tests that we forget real life doesn't work that way. When preparing a letter, we must be able to look at it and select the words we are not certain of and check them in a dictionary or elsewhere. In the last sentence of the preceding paragraph, did you detect the three misspelled words? If you didn't, you should at least be able to detect any you are not certain of. That way you will find the three misspelled words. Train your child in this skill.

3. Good spelling begins with good pronunciation. When your child learns new words, be sure she pronounces them correctly. If she says pitcher for picture or libary for library, she will have trouble spelling these words.

4. Good spelling should be made easy. In other words, it is all right to tell a child how to spell a word instead of always sending her to the dictionary. This, again, is how we operate in real life. We avoid the dictionary if anyone around us knows the word we need. This real-life system speeds up learning, encourages the child to use a wider variety of words in her writing, and keeps her on friendlier terms with the dictionary.

Where do the words in a spelling book come from? Is there magic in these lists that will turn a second grader into a third grader? If you understand where the words come from you will decide that there is more magic in the natural method of teaching spelling and writing. There are two basic approaches used in spelling books and you can borrow something from each.

The Common-Word Approach to Spelling

Spelling researchers have listed all the words people write in daily memos, letters and other ordinary writing. They count and categorize these words and find that *the* is used six or more times for every hundred words of writing, while *and*, *of*, and *to* are used about three times each. In fact, only nine words make up twenty-five percent of the words written. Fifty common words make up fifty percent of our writing and one thousand words make up more than ninety percent.

Some spelling books, then, present weekly lists of these common words. The theory is that children should learn the words which will be most useful to them. By using the natural method of writing, you teach the same words that are in these books. That is, if the books truly do contain the words children read and write, your child will meet them in her reading and writing. And you can teach them in meaningful context rather than in artificial lists.

If you wish to check out your young pupils on the most common of the common words, here are two lists to help you.

Words which make up 25% of written language

a, and, I, of, in, that, the, to, you

Words which make up the next 25% of written language

all	from	me	this
an	had	my	very
are	has	not	was
as	have	on	we
at	he	one	were
be	her	or	which
been	his	she	will
but	if	so	with
by	is	there	would
dear	it	they	your
for			

For older pupils, it is helpful to learn these fourteen prefixes.

ab (from)	dis (apart)	in (into)	sub (under)
ad (to)	en (in)	pre (before)	un (not)
be (by)	ex (out)	pro (in front of)	
com (with)	in (not)	re (back)	

The Phonics Approach to Spelling

Some spelling books are planned around phonics. An early list may have mat, cat, hat, and so forth. A later list may have might, fight, and right. Words are learned in groups according to phonics elements found in them.

In these books an important element is spelling rules—generalizations that apply to the use of letters, syllables, and affixes. Much controversy has arisen about which rules are really useful. If a rule has too many exceptions, is it worth teaching? Some people say No. And others say that in such a case you should just teach another rule which explains the exceptions.

Your child learns many spelling rules as she learns phonics. For instance, if a word starts with the same sound as *boy* she knows it starts with *b*. Most spelling rules fall into this category; they are so obvious that we hardly think of them as spelling rules.

Other rules are so complex or obscure that it is simpler to learn the words than the rules. For example, some systems teach that *ough* has six sounds: as in though, thought, enough, cough, through, and bough. "Rule" teachers would have children memorize the six sounds and try them in order when they meet a new word. "Word" teachers would figure that once children know a few of these words they will be able to decipher others when they meet them.

A child who learns to read by phonics already knows the consonants that have only one sound. She also knows those which have two or more sounds and which sometimes are silent. She knows the major sounds of the vowels and the sounds of most two- and three-letter combinations, such as *th*, *ck*, *ea*, and *ear*. Those basic phonics generalizations take care of spelling the majority of words.

By teaching a few additional spelling rules, you can insure that your child will be able to spell over ninety percent of words simply by phonics and spelling rules. Here are some rules with high utility.

    1. *I* before *e* except after *c* or when sounding like *a* as in neighbor and weigh. This works often.

    2. For *k* sound, use *k* before *e* and *i*. Use *c* before other vowels. (Cat, keg, kit, cot, cut.)

    3. Change *y* to *i* and add *es*. This rhythmic rule we have all memorized works when there is a consonant before the *y*, as in baby or city.

    4. Drop a silent *e* before endings which start with a vowel, but keep the silent *e* before endings which start with a consonant. Examples: baking, bakes.

    5. In one-syllable words with a final, single consonant, double the consonant before an ending which begins with a vowel. Examples: running, hitting. (This and Rule 4 are how you tell that hopping comes from hop, while hoping comes from hope.) The rule also applies to longer words when the last syllable is accented. Examples: expel, expelling; but worship, worshiping.

    6. Follow *q* with *u* in all common English words. In some brand names and newly coined words, this and other spelling rules are purposely violated, probably because people want to form unique words. (Examples are the double *x* in Exxon, the solitary *q* in Compaq, and the final *c* in pac.)

Personalized Spelling Approach

If the preceding sections have convinced you that spelling curriculums are not as neat we would like, you probably will feel quite comfortable teaching your child by a personalized spelling approach. This borrows from both the traditional approaches but relies mostly on daily copying and dictation work. It branches out from there as you see a need.

When your child misspells a word, you can teach it then and there.

Have her look at the model to see the difference and to correct her writing. Often that is all the help needed.

Or converse with her about why the word is spelled this way, what will help her remember it, and such. This is called "incidental teaching," which means teaching incident by incident as occasions arise. This is efficient learnng, requiring far less time than classroom style weekly spelling lists.

Other times you may notice that a particular phonics item or spelling rule may help. In such a case you can tailor a lesson or lessons to teach that.

And still other times, you may wish to fall back to the classroom list method, but individualize by gathering your own lists of words that your child needs to know. Each list should be short, just five or six words, because the child needs to learn all of them, which is seldom the case in textbook lists. A common way to use lists is to study and talk about the words, take practice tests, study more, and then on Friday take a final test. Any word missed on Friday can be carried over to the next week's list. Don't do this every week of the year, just now and then so it adds variety and change of pace to the child's language learning.

Reversing the above procedure can achieve instant learning. That is, instead of testing last, give a test first, on two or three words. Let the child see what mistakes she made, and then dictate the same words again. This is highly effective if used every once in a while on important words your child needs, but it is less effective if used too often.

In summary, personalized spelling uses these three methods.

1. On-the-spot, quick teaching in the context of a writing lesson, using mainly conversation about a word.

2. Individually tailored phonics or spelling-rule lessons.

3. Personal spelling lists

Personalized spelling is extremely efficient. Children spend study time only on words they need, not on generalized lists planned for whole classes.

In the primary grades, as explained earlier, it is best to focus on reading and writing, and let spelling take a back seat for a time to avoid overload. So the spelling ideas suggested here are to be used from time to time as seems good to you, and they should not be made into a heavy, formalized course of study separate from other language learning.

Sample Lessons

These sample lesson ideas show something of the wide range of learning levels you can meet when you use the natural method. If a child is just learning phonics, begin with one-line selections—shorter than those given here. Call attention to short vowel sounds, vowel pairs, rhymes, and so forth. If a child knows phonics and is a pretty good speller, then call attention to sentence structure, grammar, punctuation, and other such matters. And don't neglect questions which require thinking about the meaning. These sample lessons, and the method itself can be started in the primary grades, but their use should continue for years afterward. Remember that even adult writers find it an effective study method.

It is not necessary to use every idea given with these selections. You are the teacher, so pick and choose what will interest your child and profit him. Also, it is not necessary to study a selection in only one sitting. Sometimes spread a lesson over two or more days. For instance, on the first day you and your pupil may read a selection and talk about it. On the second day he could copy it, or review and write from dictation. Then he should compare and correct his copy. On the third day you could teach some grammar knowledge or thinking skill, study difficult words, and so forth, and then dictate again. When a child wants to do original writing, that takes still more time.

The goal is to help children think and learn. If that is happening, whether you race through many selections or ponder on a few, matters not at all.

If children of different ages are being tutored together they can often study the same selection. One could copy while the other writes from dictation. One could learn to spell words while the other learns grammar. One could write a shorter portion than the other. Children can dictate to each other and edit each other's papers.

These lessons are meant to be only samples. Try some and then move on to find selections yourself. Your home and your library have more than enough for a lifetime of learning. Correlate language study with other subjects by selecting from history, civics, science, and all kinds of content. Usually it is better to select from "real books" rather than textbooks.

Have the children practice neat printing for at least two years. In third grade they can begin cursive writing. Some older children do well typing or word processing their assignments.

With regular study of this kind, children gain the feel of fine writing in their bones. A bonus for you as teacher is that you will learn too. There is no end to improving command of language.

1

Jack Sprat could eat no fat.
His wife could eat no lean.
And so, between them both
They licked the platter clean.

Mother Goose

What makes these lines look like a poem? Which two lines are indented? Write all the lines from dictation or from memory. Compare yours with the model. Did you make it look like a poem? Did you spell all the words right? Which two lines have end rhymes? (The indented ones—lines two and four.) Find vowel rhymes within line one (Jack Sprat, fat). Find vowel rhymes in line three (so, both). Find out the meaning of *lean*, if you are not sure of it. If you were illustrating this rhyme, which person would you draw thin and which would you draw fat? Why?

2

One, two, three, four, five,
Once I caught a fish alive.
Six, seven, eight, nine, ten,
But I let it go again.

Mother Goose

Write from dictation, one line at a time. Did you spell all the number names right? What is the hardest number to spell? What rhymes with *five*? What rhymes with *ten*? Can you think of more rhymes for either of these? What consonants are silent in the word *caught*? Spell *caught* orally. Write it. Now write the whole poem again from dictation or from memory. Poems like this are sometimes called "nonsense rhymes." Why does that name fit? Could you think up a nonsense rhyme to help a little child learn his numbers?

3

One day a hungry fox jumped up to steal a big bunch
of purple grapes. The fox jumped and jumped, but the
grapes were too high. He could not reach them. At last
the fox said, "I can see that those grapes are sour." This
story shows that it is easy to hate what you cannot
have.

Aesop's Fables

Write from dictation. Compare your copy with the model and make
any corrections needed. Write again from dictation today or tomorrow.
Explain why the quotation marks are used as they are. Find all the
words with short *u* sound. Have you heard anyone call something
"sour grapes" when they were not talking about actual grapes? Watch
for the next few days to see if you or someone else makes a "sour
grapes" remark.

4

Samuel looked at the first son. He was a fine and
good-looking man. But the Lord said, "No, Samuel. This
is not the one."

Samuel looked at seven sons. But each time the Lord
said, "No, Samuel. This is not the the one."

Then Samuel asked, "Do you have another son?"

"Yes," said the father. "David is in the field keeping
sheep."

When David came the Lord said, "This is the one." So
Samuel poured oil on David to make him the next
king.

Adapted from I Samuel 16:6–13

Does the Lord look at the outside of a person? Where does He look?
See if you can find out more about the boy David. What punctuation
mark follows the word *No*? Read those sentences aloud and see if you
can explain why the commas are there. Explain why some of the
quotation marks are there. Write from dictation, listening carefully for
the comma pauses and the period stops. Try to get everything correct.

5

Henry Huggins' dog Ribsy was a plain ordinary city dog. He followed Henry and his friends to school. He kept the mailman company. He wagged his tail at the milkman, who always stopped to pet him. People liked Ribsy, and Ribsy liked people.

Ribsy by Beverly Cleary

Why is *Ribsy* capitalized? Why isn't *dog* capitalized? Why does an apostrophe follow Huggins? (It shows belonging, or possession.) Write from dictation.

6

The sun was just ready to go down behind the mountains, and Heidi sat quietly on the ground, gazing at the bluebells glowing in the evening light. All the grass seemed tinted with gold, and the cliffs above began to gleam and sparkle. Suddenly Heidi jumped up.

"Peter, it's on fire! It's on fire!" she exclaimed. Oh, the beautiful fiery snow!

Adapted from *Heidi*
by Johanna Spyri

Find words that help paint a pretty picture. Find *it's* two places. The apostrophe in each stands for a missing letter. What is missing? Why do you think exclamation marks are used? Copy from the model, making sure to copy indentation and quotation marks accurately. Write from dictation.

7

Mark tore the sandwiches into chunks and held them
in his hand. Ben lifted the pieces so deftly Mark scarcely
felt his tongue. The bear ate them with a great smacking
of lips. When it was all gone, Ben pushed at his hand,
looking for more. Mark gave him the empty sack, and
Ben ripped it apart, snorting and huffing at the aroma
that remained.

Gentle Ben by Walt Morey

Copy this paragraph. Check your work. Who is the subject of the
first sentence? Who is the subject of the third sentence? Find words
that tell what Ben did (ate, ripped and others). Action words like these
are called *verbs*. Find verbs that tell what Mark did. Do you think the
verbs in this story help to make it interesting? Tell why or why not.
Tomorrow write from dictation.

8

He was a mongoose, rather like a little cat in his fur
and his tail, but quite like a weasel in his head and his
habits. His eyes and the end of his restless nose were
pink. He could fluff up his tail till it looked like a bottle
brush, and his war cry, as he scuttled through the long
grass, was: "Rikk-tikk-tikki-tikki-tchk!"

Rikki-Tikki-Tavi by Rudyard Kipling

Study the war cry to see how Rudyard Kipling spelled it. Then write
this paragraph from dictation. Compare yours with the model. Be
especially careful to check the commas. Could any comma be a period
instead and still leave complete sentences? (Only the one after *brush*.)
If Kipling had made two sentences out of this, what would be the subject of each? (He, cry.) The verb of each? (Could fluff, was.) Explain
why the other sentences could not be cut in two without changing any
words. A sentence that can be cut in two is called a compound sentence; it has a subject and its verb in each part.

9

The sun isn't solid, as the earth is. It is a huge, lumpy, flaming ball, made mostly of the gases hydrogen and helium. When the sun, which is a star, is compared to other stars, the sun is only medium-sized. Compared to earth, the sun is very big. More than a million earths could fit inside it.

Putting the Sun to Work by Jeanne Bendick

Put the words of the fourth sentence in a different order to make another sentence that tells the same thing. Study the commas after huge and lumpy. Can you make up a rule for using commas like this? (Put a comma after each item in a list.) Copy or write from dictation.

10

When Tom reached the schoolhouse, he strode in briskly, with the manner of one who had come with all honest speed. He hung his hat on a peg and flung himself into his seat with businesslike alacrity. The master, throned on high in his great splint-bottomed armchair, was dozing, lulled by the drowsy hum of study. The interruption roused him.

"Thomas Sawyer! Why are you late again?"

Tom Sawyer by Mark Twain

Copy the model. Tell who is speaking in the quotation. How do you know? Write the third sentence in brief form with just the simple subject and verb. Add *The* for a better sounding sentence. (The master was dozing.) Does that give you a mental image of what happened? How did Mark Twain add more to the image? Write the first two sentences also, as briefly as you can, and add the fourth sentence, which is already brief. Read the four short sentences aloud. Listen as someone else reads them. Now read Mark Twain's original paragraph aloud, or listen to it. Do you see any reason why people have loved Mark Twain's writings for so long? If you do, try to explain. Tomorrow, write the passage from dictation.

11

Do you know that the calendar is in the sky? Few people do. To know the real story behind the neat little calendars we use today, we must find out how the very ancient people made their timetables according to the stars and the moon and the sun. All sorts of mistakes were made before the ancient scientists devised a calendar system that was nearly right.

Our Calendar by Ruth Brindze

Find a word that is made of two words. This is called a compound word. Find the shortest sentence. Find the longest sentence. In good writing, sentence length varies like this. Write from dictation.

12

After the Constitutional Convention ended, many people were not sure what had been accomplished. The story goes that a lady went up to Benjamin Franklin. "Well, doctor, what have we got," she asked, "a republic or a monarchy?"

The wise old statesman answered simply, "A republic—if you can keep it."

The Office of President
by James McCague

Find out what the Constitutional Convention was. Break these two long words into parts, called syllables. Spell each syllable. Then spell the whole words. Repeat this kind of study with other long words. What do you think Franklin meant by his answer? Ask some grownups what they think he meant. Write this from dictation. Repeat one or more times if you misspell words or make other mistakes.

13

"Uncle!" I cried. "I've got a fish."

"Not yet," said my uncle.

As he spoke there was a splash in the water, and I caught the gleam of a scared fish shooting into the middle of the stream. My hook hung empty from the line. I had lost my prize.

"Remember, boy," my uncle said, with his shrewd smile, "never brag of catching a fish until he is on dry ground."

John Greenleaf Whittier

Write from dictation without studying beforehand. Can you get the paragraphing and punctuation correct? What do you think Uncle could say next if he wanted to teach John a lesson about life? (People shouldn't brag about anything before it's done. And after it's done there is no need to brag because the action speaks for itself.) Explain why, in the last paragraph, the second part of the quotation does not start with a capital letter. If you could do better on a second try, write this from dictation again tomorrow.

14

I proposed to my brother that if he would give me, weekly, half the money he paid for my board, I would board myself. He instantly agreed to it, and I presently found that I could save half what he paid me. This was an additional fund for buying of books. But I had another advantage in it. My brother and the rest going from the printing house to their meals, I remained there alone, and, dispatching presently my light repast, I had the rest of the time till their return for study.

The Autobiography of Benjamin Franklin

What do you learn about Benjamin Franklin from this paragraph? What is the meaning of board in this paragraph? If you're not sure, ask somebody. Notice the phrase, "dispatching presently my light repast." If you were writing this, what words might you use instead? Are there other phrases you would like to change? If so, try rewriting the whole paragraph your way. Check your writing carefully. Edit and correct it until there are no mistakes. Now see if you can write Franklin's paragraph from dictation.

Bible Sentences for Writing Practice

These fifty sentences provide practice with over one hundred fifty most commonly used words. Some common words are not very simple phonetically—such as brought, sure, eyes, love. So children may not be able to sound them out, and it helps to teach such words in the context of a sentence.

Writing these sentences will do much more for children than help them learn spelling, penmanship, and sentence structure. The beauty and wisdom of Bible words will shape their minds and hearts. The majestic sound, the simplicity, the fine rhythm will develop their ears for excellent language. A child who grows into English using the Bible regularly will always be a better writer and thinker because of it. Children may use these sentences and other Bible portions of your choice from age five to age ten or more.

Beginners. First, you should make a model in neat printing for the young child to copy. If it takes him several minutes to copy "I love the Lord," you should have lessons for several days on the same sentence. After learning to copy it, the child should learn to print it from dictation as you say or spell the words for him. Next, he should learn to print it without any help in spelling, capitalizing or punctuating. Then it is time to choose a new sentence to master by the same steps. Each sentence will be easier to learn than the last.

Advanced. Older children will be able to write several sentences from dictation in one sitting. They may also check their writing against the models and learn from their mistakes.

In-Between. Between the beginners and the advanced sentence writers are the children who will profit most from this kind of practice. With these children, let them first copy a sentence or write it from slow dictation, while you give all the help with spelling and other matters that they need, so the writing is correct. In subsequent lessons, repeat the same sentence until the children can write correctly after you dictate it with proper expression.

Children at all levels may not completely understand some details, such as semicolons, but that's all right. At least they are meeting and seeing these elements at work in sentences. Later on they will understand better. That is the way of learning: some things we know well, some things we sort of know, and some things we have just been introduced to for the first time. All the learning grows together. This is why "whole" learning works so efficiently. Whole sentences, whole paragraphs, whole stories—these are the route to good writing, speaking and thinking.

In the Bible (KJV) sentences which follow, a few adjustments have been made to adapt them for language teaching. For instance, *you* is used in place of *ye*, and *makes* is used in place of *maketh*. Spelling, also, conforms to present American usage. For instance, *forever* is spelled as one word instead of two.

The sentences provide a variety of noble thoughts—praise, prayer, admonition and choice wisdom in both prose and poetry. You need not use sentences in the order presented here. And you may sometimes insert selections made by you or your pupils.

Do not have children write the references. These are included in the list in case you want to look up more information about a sentence, or if a child wants to do a creative writing assignment about one of the sentences. Also, do not use this list for memory assignments and spend a lot of time memorizing "addresses" of the verses. This language learning should focus on writing, meaning, and character building—not on addresses.

Here are ideas to use in your lessons with these sentences. They are listed in order from easy to hard.

1. Let the child either **copy** from a model or **write** from slow dictation in which you give all the help needed to get a correct copy. Use copying or dictation methods according to the child's preference. Have the child read from his copy.

2. Let the child **study** a sentence model and then write it from dictation, or from memory if he knows it. Note his mistakes, if any, and help him learn from them. Dictate again, using proper sentence expression. Have the child **read** from his copy.

3. Let the child study and write as in 2, above. Have the child **proofread** his copy to assure that it is the best he can do. Then have him **compare** with the model and find any mistakes. Dictate again, using good sentence expression. Or if the child knows it well enough, he may write from memory. Read. Compare.

4. **Dictate** a sentence the child has not seen. On the first dictation, read the sentence whole with good expression. Repeat readings may break it down into smaller parts if necessary. Compare. Dictate again.

5. Dictate a sentence whole. Repeat as needed, but always make it sound like a whole sentence. Compare the child's writing with the model. Dictate again.

6. **Review.**

7. Dictate three or four sentences, one at a time. Compare with the models. Dictate again the ones that do not match the models. This assignment is easier if the child gets to look at the models first, and harder if he does not see them first. Sometimes try it the easy way, and sometimes the harder way.

8. For an occasional **creative writing** assignment, have the child write a paragraph, story, or essay about one of the sentences. He may tell in his own words what it means. He may tell who in the Bible said it, who it was spoken to, and what the circumstances were. He may give an example of how someone could live by the words in modern life. He may make up a story of someone living by the words today. Or he may use an idea of his own for writing. Always talk about this assignment for a time. Help the child get some ideas for writing before he has to start. If you or the pupil can't come up with some good ideas, you'd better choose another subject.

List of Bible Sentences

Easy

I love the Lord. *(Psalm 116:1)*

Love one another. *(I John 4:7)*

Let us love one another, for love is of God. *(I John 4:7)*

Be kind one to another. *(Ephesians 4:32)*

You must be born again. *(John 3:7)*

Medium

You believe in God, believe also in me. *(John 14:1)*

But many that are first shall be last; and the last shall be first. *(Matthew 19:30)*

Your Father knows what things you have need of, before you ask him. *(Matthew 6:8)*

God has given him a name which is above every name. *(Philippians 2:9)*

The heavens are the work of your hands. *(Psalm 102:25)*

My help comes from the Lord, which made heaven and earth. *(Psalm 121:2)*

I will dwell in the house of the Lord forever. *(Psalm 23:6)*

The Lord is a great God, and a great king. *(Psalm 95:3)*

Show me your ways, O Lord; teach me your paths. *(Psalm 25:4)*

Ask for the old paths, where is the good way, and walk therein. *(Jeremiah 6:16)*

How much better is it to get wisdom than gold! *(Proverbs 16:16)*

A wise son hears his father's instruction. *(Proverbs 13:1)*

And you shall do that which is right and good in the sight of the Lord. *(Deuteronomy 6:18)*

The rich and poor meet together: the Lord is the maker of them all. *(Proverbs 22:2)*

And God said, Let there be light: and there was light. *(Genesis 1:3)*

Have you an arm like God?
Or can you thunder with a voice like him?
(Job 40:9)

O God, you are my God; early will I seek you. *(Psalm 63:1)*

Every man shall give as he is able. *(Deuteronomy 16:17)*

You shall truly tithe year by year. *(Deuteronomy 14:22)*

They are the eyes of the Lord, which run to and fro through the whole earth. *(Zechariah 4:10)*

I will take you to me for a people, and I will be to you a God. *(Exodus 6:7)*

They that seek the Lord shall not want any good thing. *(Psalm 34:10)*

Be sure your sin will find you out. *(Numbers 32:23)*

Blessed are the pure in heart: for they shall see God. *(Matthew 5:8)*

Little children, keep yourselves from idols. *(I John 5:21)*

It is not good that the man should be alone. *(Genesis 2:18)*

Therefore shall a man leave his father and his mother, and shall cleave unto his wife. *(Genesis 2:24)*

The love of money is the root of all evil. *(I Timothy 6:10)*

As far as the east is from the west, so far has he removed our sins from us. *(Psalm 103:12)*

We walked unto the house of God in company. *(Psalm 55:14)*

And whosoever was not found written in the book of life was cast into the lake of fire. *(Revelation 20:15)*

And whosoever will, let him take the water of life freely. *(Revelation 22:17)*

You are the light of the world. A city that is set on a hill cannot be hid. *(Matthew 5:14)*

Because I live, you shall live also. *(John 14:19)*

If a man keep my saying, he shall never taste of death. *(John 8:52)*

I am the door: by me if any man enter in, he shall be saved. *(John 10:9)*

The thought of foolishness is sin. *(Proverbs 24:9)*

And as you would that men should do to you, do you also to them likewise. *(Luke 6:31)*

Weeping may endure for a night, but joy comes in the morning. *(Psalm 30:5)*

Difficult

For there is one God, and one mediator between God and men, the man Christ Jesus. *(I Timothy 2:5)*

And there are also many other things which Jesus did, the which, if they should be written every one, I suppose that even the world itself could not contain the books that should be written. *(John 21:25)*

You, whose name alone is Jehovah, are the most high over all the earth. *(Psalm 83:18)*

So teach us to number our days, that we may apply our hearts unto wisdom. *(Psalm 90:12)*

For if a man think himself to be something, when he is nothing, he deceives himself. *(Galatians 6:3)*

Eye has not seen, nor ear heard, neither have entered into the heart of man, the things which God has prepared for them that love him. *(I Corinthians 2:9)*